William and Dorothy
The Dove Cottage Years
1799–1808

JONATHAN WORDSWORTH

The Wordsworth Trust Grasmere

Compiled from essays written originally for
the Friends of Dove Cottage annual leaflet
First published in book form 1987 by
The Wordsworth Trust
Dove Cottage, Grasmere, Cumbria LA22 95G

ISBN 0 9510616 4 X

Typeset by Gloucester Typesetting Services
and printed in Great Britain by
The Roundwood Press
Kineton, Warwick CV35 0HW

Cover design, *Sampler*, Josefina Alys Hermes de Vasconcellos

Inside cover, doves feeding, is thought to be by John Ruskin

William and Dorothy always hoped one day to set up house together. Their early childhood, spent at Cockermouth with their three brothers, was close and happy; but when William was eight, and Dorothy seven, their mother died. Dorothy was sent away to live with relatives, and for many years they were separated. At last, in the autumn of 1795 – when they were both in their mid-twenties – they were lent a house at Racedown, in Dorset. It was the first home that they had had.

By this stage, William had been to Cambridge, and published two poems – one about the Lake District, the other about a walking-tour in the Alps in 1790. On a second visit to France, in 1791–2, he had become an active supporter of the Revolution; he had also fallen in love, and become the father of a child (whose mother, Annette Vallon, he was not to meet again until 1802, because of the war between their countries).

By summer 1797, when they left Racedown so as to be near Coleridge at Alfoxden in Somerset, William had written *The Ruined Cottage*. His Great Decade had begun. In the year that followed, Coleridge produced his three most famous poems, *Kubla Khan*, *The Ancient Mariner* and the first part of *Christabel*; William wrote his Lyrical Ballads and *Tintern Abbey*; Dorothy composed the first of her *Journals* that tell of their companionship, and the day-to-day life from which the poetry emerged.

The winter of 1798–9 was spent in Germany, where William wrote the haunting Lucy Poems, and the first drafts of his great autobiography, *The Prelude*, taking us back in vivid detail to the scenes of his boyhood, when he had hung

> Above the raven's nest, by knots of grass
> Or half-inch fissures in the slippery rock . . .

A year later they were living at Dove Cottage amid these very scenes.

Grasmere, c. 1800: Harriet Green (Abbot Hall, Kendal).

The earliest known picture of Dove Cottage: Amos Green, 1735–1807 (Wordsworth Museum).

1799

William and Dorothy Wordsworth arrived at Dove Cottage by post-chaise from Kendal at 4.30 on the afternoon of 20 December 1799. Molly Fisher, who lived over the road at Sykeside, has left us a vivid picture of Dorothy standing in front of the parlour fire on that first evening, in her 'laal striped gown' and 'laal straw bonnet'. William was 29, and Dorothy was going to be 28 on Christmas Day. They had crossed the country, partly on horseback, partly on foot, from Sockburn in County Durham, where they had been staying with Mary Hutchinson, whom Wordsworth married three years later in October 1802. Dove Cottage was to be their home until 1808, when it became finally too small for the growing family.

But it was more than a home: it was a dream come true. As a schoolboy, rambling over from Hawkshead, William had once looked down on Grasmere from the top of Red Bank, and the vale lived on in his mind:

> From that time forward was the place to me
> As beautiful in thought as it had been
> When present to my bodily eyes . . .

We cannot know when he and Dorothy had first dreamed of sharing a cottage, but it became their dearest wish. Since autumn 1795 they had been together in a succession of temporary homes. Now they were to have a place of their own.

To William, in March 1800, it seemed that paradise had been achieved. 'This solitude is mine', he wrote exultantly,

> the distant thought
> Is fetched out of the heaven in which it was:
> The unappropriated bliss hath found
> An owner, and that owner I am he!

Adam himself could not have been so happy! How could there be true fulfilment 'Among the bowers / Of blissful Eden', when there had been no period of yearning, nothing to long for?

Though William and Dorothy might think of it as paradise, Dove Cottage had been built as a pub – the Dove and Olive Bough. It was more substantial than the neighbouring cottages of Town End, and as one came through the door a touch of dignity was offered by the panelling. A charming picture of the Wordsworths' first four days in the house is offered by William, writing to Coleridge on Christmas Eve.

Dorothy 'has so much work for her needle among the bedcurtains &c that she is absolutely buried in it'. She also has toothache, but nothing has stopped her getting out and planning things in the garden:

in imagination she has already built a seat with a summer shed on the highest platform in this our little domestic slip of mountain. The spot commands a view over the roof of our house, of the lake, the church, Helm Cragg, and two thirds of the vale. We mean also to enclose the two or three yards of ground between us and the road, this for the sake of a few flowers, and because it will make it more our own.

For all the newfound joys of ownership, the Wordsworths did not feel that they could hug their good fortune entirely to themselves. In coming to this tiny northern village, 250 miles from London, they were not opting out. Throughout his life, William remained passionately interested in public affairs. But he had his own vocation, and he took it very seriously. He was going to write poetry that would make the world a better place.

1800

1800 set the pattern of the Wordsworths' life at Dove Cottage – the visits from Coleridge and others; the walks; the fishing and bathing and boating; the frequent readings of poetry; William's composition, sometimes in the house, more often pacing out-of-doors; Dorothy's copying for her brother, and keeping for him the *Journal* that tells us so faithfully the details of their loving, domestic, productive existence:

Thursday 31 July 1800. All the morning I was busy copying poems. Gathered peas, and in the afternoon Coleridge came, very hot ... The men went to bathe, and we afterwards sailed down to Loughrigg. Read poems on the water, and let the boat take its own course. We walked a long time upon Loughrigg, and returned in the grey twilight. The moon just setting as we reached home.

William must have begun writing as soon as they arrived in Grasmere. The first Dove Cottage poems, *The Brothers* and *Hart-Leap Well*, were finished in February, leaving him free to begin *The Recluse* – the great philo-sophical poem which he had planned with Coleridge in Somerset, and which he thought of as his life's work. *Home at Grasmere*, begun in early March, was intended to be Book One; but in place of the public voice, we hear a ten-der, personal thanksgiving. Here he was, as he had always hoped to be, sharing with Dorothy in this beautiful vale the way of life they had long ago chosen:

> Mine eyes did ne'er
> Rest on a lovely object, nor my mind
> Take pleasure in the midst of happy thoughts,
> But either she whom now I have, who now
> Divides with me this loved abode, was there
> Or not far off. Where'er my footsteps turned

> Her voice was like a hidden bird that sang,
> The thought of her was like a flash of light
> Or an unseen companionship, a breath
> Or fragrance independent of the wind . . .

The first three visitors to stay at Dove Cottage were, appropriately: William and Dorothy's sailor brother, John, who came in January and spent eight very happy months before taking command of the *Earl of Aber-gavenny* (in which, sadly, he was drowned five years later); Mary Hutchinson, who came the next month, and was to marry William in October 1802; and Coleridge, whose visit in April led to the reprinting of *Lyrical Ballads*, with a new, second volume. Coleridge came back again in June, and in July moved his family up from the south to Greta Hall in Keswick. To William and Dorothy, the twelve rugged miles between Keswick and Grasmere seemed nothing, and Coleridge—despite his opium and his illness – would at times lengthen the journey by coming over Helvellyn!

The summer and autumn of 1800 were extremely active. There was revision and copying to do for *Lyrical Ballads*; there was composition of the famous Preface (described by Coleridge in 1802 as 'half the child of my own brain'); and there was new work from each of the poets. Coleridge produced the second part of *Christabel*, but couldn't bring his poem to an end. Something had to fill the space reserved for it in *Lyrical Ballads*. Writ-ing at great speed, Wordsworth composed his tragic story of the Grasmere shepherd, Michael, basing it upon a sheepfold which he and Dorothy had found on 11 October, 'Beside the boisterous brook of Greenhead Gill'.

Coleridge's house, Greta Hall, on top of its wooded hill at Keswick: William Westall, 1820 (Wordsworth Museum).

The East Indiaman, Earl of Abergavenny, on which the poet's brother, John Wordsworth, made five voyages, the last three as commander: Thomas Luny, 1801 (British Library: India Office Records).

Dorothy Wordsworth's account of meeting the leech-gatherer on 3 October 1800 (Wordsworth Library).

Charles James Fox, Leader of the Opposition, to whom Wordsworth sent 'Lyrical Ballads', 1800, and whose death he lamented in 'Loud is the Vale': K. A. Hichel, *c.* 1793 (National Portrait Gallery).

1801

Among the new poems that made up the second volume of *Lyrical Ballads*, *The Brothers* and *Michael*, both composed at Dove Cottage, had a special importance for Wordsworth. They had been written, he told the Whig Leader, Charles James Fox, when sending him a copy of the book in January 1801, 'with a view to show that men who do not wear fine clothes can feel deeply'.

The life of the Lake District 'statesmen' – sheep-farmers who worked their own small properties on the sides of the mountains – had come to seem an ideal. In *Michael* the old shepherd has a depth of feeling for his land and for his family that is born out of ownership and pride in the work that he and Isabel share. His affections, as Wordsworth points out to Fox, would be inconceivable to those familiar only with 'hired labourers and the manufacturing poor'. To some extent Michael is a 'silent poet', like the Wordsworths' sailor brother, John, who was staying at Dove Cottage when the poem was written; but mainly he stands for the happiness that may be attained in an honest, hard-working, independent life, lived in harmony with the surrounding natural world.

The existence that William and Dorothy shared at Dove Cottage was no less dedicated. They believed passionately that just as Michael and Isabel's lamp, shining out over the vale, had become 'a public symbol of the life / The thrifty pair had lived', so William's poetry might be

> Even as a light hung up in heaven to cheer
> The world in times to come.

This belief was at the centre of everything they did. Dorothy was not just William's housekeeper, and constant tenderly-loved companion, she was his secretary, kept hard at work copying and recopying his manuscripts to keep pace with the revisions. Even her *Journals* were shared, providing on important occasions material for the poetry.

By modern standards their existence was very frugal. Not only did they not wear fine clothes, they were grateful that John before setting out on his voyage in spring 1801 should send William all the old ones he could muster. There were very few luxuries at Dove Cottage. In a letter of February, William reveals that he has not bought, or even seen, a new book since they came to Grasmere thirteen months before. He refuses an invitation to Yorkshire on the grounds that he is 'not strong enough to walk' (he had been ill), 'and too poor to ride', and goes on to describe his and Dorothy's 'very homely fare – no wine, and even little beer.' It was an exciting moment when in April a second cousin sent them 'a barrel of the best flour from America.'

In some ways of course they were privileged. Thanks to the legacy he had received in 1795 from his wealthy friend, Raisley Calvert (who believed in him as a poet, and wished to make him independent), William had never had to take a job. And Dorothy did have help in the house. Old Molly Fisher was not at all competent, but she repaid Dorothy's patience by being a warm and devoted presence. To her we owe the entry in the *Journal* that tells us first of William's engagement to Mary Hutchinson:

Molly has been very witty with Mary all day. She says 'Ye may say what ye will but there's nothing like a gay auld man for behaving weel to a young wife . . .'

One wonders how old William seemed. In truth he and Mary were both 31.

1802

It was William Cowper, the poet whom Wordsworth so often resembles, who spoke of domestic happiness as 'the only bliss / Of Paradise that has survived the Fall'. The companionship of William and Dorothy during spring 1802 has just this quality. At times their happiness was troubled by anxiety over Coleridge, whose life at Keswick was so sadly different from their own, but for the most part these were months of unruffled pleasure – both in each other, and in their surroundings. The mood is captured by Dorothy's account of a walk by Brothers Water:

There was the gentle flowing of the stream, the glittering lively lake, green fields without a living creature to be seen on them, behind us a flat pasture with 42 cattle feeding. . . . The people were at work ploughing, harrowing and sowing – lasses spreading dung, a dog's barking now and then, cocks crowing, birds twittering, the snow in patches at the top of the highest hills . . .

Few writers have been able to bring before us so vividly the feelings of the English countryside. William too was in a jubilant mood. The details that Dorothy had noticed are turned at once into a song of triumph at the coming of spring:

> The cock is crowing,
> The stream is flowing,
> The small birds twitter,
> The lake doth glitter,
> The green field sleeps in the sun . . .
> The cattle are grazing,
> Their heads never raising;
> There are forty feeding like one!

Coleridge's marriage was, in his own words, 'exceedingly miserable'. He was in love with Sara Hutchinson, sister of William's future wife, but could not think of divorce. His health and his opium-addiction got steadily worse. While William was writing poem after poem, he felt his own creativity to be deadened by unhappiness. When he did put pen to paper, it was to write a verse-letter to Sara evoking in beautiful but distressing poetry his sense of being cut off from the joys at Grasmere. No wonder that Dorothy was 'in miserable spirits' when, five days after her walk by 'the glittering lively lake', Coleridge came and read them *Dejection*. 'The sunshine, the green fields, and the fair sky make me sadder', she writes, with William's *Ode* in her mind, 'even the little happy sporting lambs seemed but sorrowful to me'.

1802 was also the time of the Peace of Amiens, the first truce in the war with France. William and Dorothy took the chance to visit Annette Vallon, whom he had not seen for ten years, and to meet for the first time his daughter Caroline. Annette's two surviving letters date from 1793. They are full of tenderness, and there is no doubt that she and William then expected to get married. When they met at Calais in August, however, William was engaged to Mary Hutchinson. We are left to guess what Annette's feelings may have been. They had been separated a long time, but William was the father of her child. Had she really ceased to hope?

Reading her *Journal* for 4 October, one can have no doubt that for Dorothy the marriage of William and Mary was an emotional moment. She wore the ring on her own finger the night before, and then could not bear to be present in the church. But Mary was one of her oldest and dearest friends. She never trespassed on the closeness of brother and sister. Through their long lives her companionship was a source of happiness to both.

Wyburn Water (now Thirlmere Reservoir) 1802, showing the original water-level, and the line of the Wordsworths' and Coleridge's frequent walks between Grasmere and Keswick: William Green (Jonathan Wordsworth). Picture trimmed at head.

Nineteenth-century photograph of the 'Rock of Names' beside Wyburn Water, on which the Wordsworths, Coleridge and the Hutchinson sisters, carved their initials in 1801–2. (Blown up in 1886, during the construction of Thirlmere, the 'Rock' has now been reconstituted behind the Wordsworth Museum.)

Town End, Grasmere, with Dove Cottage at the extreme right: John Wilson Carmichael 1800–68 (Wordsworth Museum).

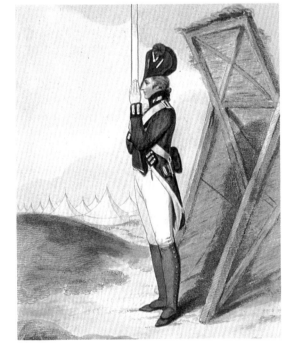

'Present arms!' – a Volunteer of the period in 'military apparel' such as Wordsworth would have worn (National Army Museum).

1803

'William had a fancy for some gingerbread', writes Dorothy on 16 January 1803:

I put on Molly's cloak . . . and we walked towards Matthew Newton's. I went into the house. The blind man and his wife and sister were sitting by the fire, all dressed very clean in their Sunday clothes, the sister reading. They took their little stock of gingerbread out of the cupboard, and I bought 6 pennyworth.

'They were so grateful', Dorothy goes on, 'that I could not find it in my heart to tell them that we were going to make gingerbread ourselves.' The Wordsworths were not rich, but with the repayment at this period of the money owed by Lord Lonsdale to their father, they could afford the occasional fancy. Their neighbours could not.

Life at Dove Cottage had not yet been greatly altered by William's marriage; change would come later in the year with the birth of Johnny, first of the five children. Dorothy's *Journal* for 11 January records what was no doubt a very typical day. William was at work on *The Prelude*; Coleridge was ill, and thinking of a trip to the Canaries; Mary and Dorothy had been reading Chaucer, and copying poems to be sent off to *The Courier* in London. As it turned out, this was not going to be a productive year for the poet, but the making and reading of literature was at the centre of all their lives. As she wrote, Dorothy was indeed making one of the best loved and most delightful works of English prose, without realising it.

Sadly for us, the *Journal* was coming to an end. In August, however, William and Dorothy set out with Coleridge on a tour of the Highlands. Dorothy's *Recollections*, written after their return, contain some of her sharpest observations – of a dropsical Scottish landlady for instance: 'she was the most cruel and even hateful-looking woman I ever saw' – and some also of her most beautiful descriptions. A lake near Dumbarton

was indeed a strange mixture of soothing and restless images, of images inviting to rest, and others hurrying the fancy away into an activity still more pleasing than repose.

At a half-way stage on the tour Coleridge went off on his own. He and William had both been moody and unwell. No clear account emerges, but a good deal can be deduced from a letter of magnificent disloyalty that Coleridge wrote to Tom Poole in October. With 'a feeling of friendly regret and disinterested apprehension' he has seen Wordsworth

more and more benetted in hypochondriacal fancies, living wholly among *devotees* – having every the minutest thing, almost his very eating and drinking, done for him by his sister, or wife . . .

The sadness and strains and envy are put into their true context by a Coleridge notebook-entry written only three weeks later: 'illness would not materially diminish my happiness if I were a housemate with love'.

No doubt there was an element of truth in Coleridge's portrait; but, hypochondriac or not, Wordsworth ended the year doing two things that his sister and wife could not do for him – writing patriotic sonnets, and drilling (in full uniform) with the Westmorland Volunteers to repel the French invasion that never came.

1804

1804 was the most productive year of Wordsworth's life. He took a rest at the time of Dora's birth in the summer, but the year began with six months of writing, and ended with another three. In all he composed eight and a half books of *The Prelude* (averaging 700 lines apiece), as well as *Ode to Duty*, the bulk of *Intimations*, *Daffodils*, and a fair number of lesser poems.

Underlying this extraordinary creativeness was anxiety for Coleridge. Opium had ruined his health, and he was going to the Mediterranean in search of a warmer climate. Though he was only 31, his friends thought he might die. William was doubly anxious – afraid for Coleridge himself, and afraid because his death would remove all possibility of help with writing *The Recluse*. News of an attack of diarrhoea which Coleridge experienced in London while waiting to set sail (and which he lovingly described to many correspondents) seemed to him 'the severest shock' he had ever received. 'I would gladly have given three fourths of my possessions', he wrote,

for your letter on *The Recluse* at that time. I cannot say what a load it would be to me, should I survive you and you die without this memorial left behind.

Coleridge didn't die, but he was never able to put on paper what he wanted *The Recluse* to say. Meanwhile, William carried on with his autobiography, which was easier to write because its philosophy didn't have to be put forward as a system. By early March he had made a version of *The Prelude* in five books for Coleridge to take with him on his voyage. Then he dismantled it again, because he couldn't bear

his task to be over, and went ahead with the full-length poem that we know. To this hectic period belong the great imaginative sequences on the Climbing of Snowdon and Crossing of the Alps, scribbled into a tiny notebook, three inches by two, that Dorothy had used in Scotland to make jottings for her *Recollections*.

'He walks out every morning', Dorothy writes in February, 'generally alone, and brings us in a large treat almost every time he goes'. A month later we hear that she and Mary have been 'making a complete copy of William's [unpublished] poems for poor Coleridge, to be his companions in Italy'. And in May she gives a fascinating account of the poet's actual habits of composition:

In wet weather he takes out an umbrella, chooses the most sheltered spot, and there walks backwards and forwards; and though the length of his walk be sometimes a quarter or half of a mile, he is as fast bound within the chosen limits as if by prison walls.

Dorothy's image of the prison is a reminder that in the middle of his work on the five-book *Prelude*, William found time to develop the four existing stanzas of *Intimations* (written in 1802) into the great final poem, with its 'shades of the prison-house', and myth of pre-existence. And in another, quite different, way it leads one to think of *Ode to Duty* – the very personal (and much neglected) poem which shows that a part of Wordsworth, amid all this creative energy, was longing for constraint:

Me this unchartered freedom tires,
I feel the weight of chance desires,
My hopes no more must change their name:
I long for a repose which ever is the same.

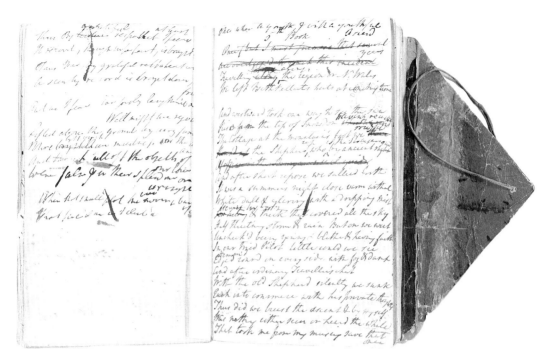

'The Climbing of Snowdon', opening of the final book of the five-book 'Prelude' of 1804 (to be used in Book XIII of the full-length poem the following year) (Wordsworth Library).

Portrait of Coleridge, made on 21 March 1804, while he was waiting in London to sail for the Mediterranean: George Dance (Wordsworth Museum).

Contemporary print, showing the wreck of John Wordsworth's ship, the Earl of Abergavenny, 5 February 1805 (Wordsworth Museum).

'Weymouth Bay', painted with the death of John Wordsworth in mind: John Constable (National Gallery).

1805

On 11 February 1805 came news that John, younger brother of William and Dorothy, had died at sea. There was a bond between John, the 'silent poet', and the family at Dove Cottage. As William put it, 'He would work for me (that was his language), for me, and his sister; and I was to endeavour to do something for the world'.

John had not only given emotional support to William in his role as poet; he had intended, by trading on his own account, to provide him and Dorothy with a settled future. His ship, the *Earl of Abergavenny*, was the largest merchant-ship in the East India Company's fleet. When she sank on the Shambles off the Dorset coast, she was on a voyage to Bengal and China that would have been profitable to her captain as well as his Company.

Not that grief over John's death had anything to do with money. He was truly loved. William could not at first bring himself to write an elegy, but by August he had written the tender muted lines of *To the Daisy*:

> Six weeks beneath the moving sea
> He lay in slumber quietly,
> Unforced by wind or wave
> To quit the ship for which he died
> (All claims of duty satisfied),
> And there they found him at her side
> And bore him to the grave.

One immediate effect of John's death seems to have been to drive William on to finishing *The Prelude*. The last three books of the poem were written very fast in April and May; but there could be little pleasure when it was completed. 'I was dejected on many accounts', the poet wrote two weeks later,

above all, many heavy thoughts of my poor departed brother hung upon me – the joy which I should have had in showing him the manuscript, and a thousand other vain fancies and dreams.

John's death made the family long especially for Coleridge's return from Malta, but he did not come for more than another year. In his absence William could not bring himself to face the long-neglected *Recluse*, but in November he had the composure to write one of the most perfect of all his lyric poems, *The Solitary Reaper*:

> Behold her, single in the field,
> Yon solitary Highland lass,
> Reaping and singing by herself –
> Stop here, or gently pass!
> Alone she cuts and binds the grain,
> And sings a melancholy strain:
> O listen, for the vale profound
> Is overflowing with the sound!

'There is something', Dorothy comments, 'inexpressibly soothing . . . in the sound of those [last] two lines'.

Looking back on Christmas Day (her thirty-fourth birthday), Dorothy is able to write: 'Six Christmases have we spent at Grasmere. . . . I think these years have been the very happiest of my life.' It is a touching scene that she paints as the children wait for their Christmas dinner, Dora 'fretful', and John (like Betty Foy) *all alive* at the thought of two plum-puddings rumbling in the pot, and a sirloin of beef that is smoking at the fire.' 'Old Molly and John Fisher', she adds, 'are in the kitchen, but when dinner is ready they are to come upstairs and partake with us'.

1806

1806 was the year of Coleridge's return from Malta – a return which was many times delayed, and finally a sad anti-climax. The year began, however, with William in a mood of unexpected jollity, telling the story of Benjamin the Waggoner and the team of horses that only he could manage on the steep road past Dove Cottage (no longer the welcoming Dove and Olive Bough) and over Dunmail Raise.

By the end of March William was in London, spending a lot of time in Grosvenor Square with Sir George Beaumont (patron of Coleridge, Constable, and others), but also meeting William Godwin, mentor of his early republican days. He was determined, he said, 'to see everything and everybody, good, bad, great, little, &c.' Robert Southey, who was there, commented unkindly:

Wordsworth flourishes in London, he powders [his hair] and goes to all the great routs. No man is more flattered by the attentions of the great, and no man would be more offended to be told so.

To this London trip belongs everyone's favourite portrait of Wordsworth, drawn by Henry Edridge, who was a society painter and quietly remodelled the poet's impressive but rather ugly features. No doubt it was another acceptable kind of flattery. But the pleasure in London and its 'routs' (fashionable parties) was masking both personal grief and a sense in Wordsworth of having changed in a deep and irrevocable way. Back in Grasmere, he recollected a Beaumont picture of Peele Castle in a storm, and wrote what is at once the most beautiful lament for John, and a farewell to his own carefree younger self:

Ah, then, if mine had been the painter's hand,
To express what then I saw – and add the gleam,
The light that never was on sea or land,
The consecration and the poet's dream –

I would have planted thee, thou hoary pile,
Amid a world how different from this,
Beside a sea that could not cease to smile,
On tranquil land, beneath a sky of bliss. . . .

So once it would have been; 'tis so no more.
I have submitted to a new control –
A power is gone which nothing can restore –
A deep distress hath humanised my soul.

Amidst the poet's grieving over John, and connected with it by intertwinings of relationship and shared experience, were fears for Coleridge. Might he too be dead? As usual, it is Dorothy who tells us how they were feeling at Dove Cottage: 'every post-day we trembled when the news was coming up stairs . . . when I was alone in bed at night I could not banish the most dreadful images'.

In the event, Coleridge reached England in August, then dallied in the south for almost ten weeks. When at last he did come north, they felt he was shutting himself off from them. Dorothy reported him 'utterly changed'. It was all painful and uneasy; but Coleridge was deeply loved, and the kindness of the Beaumonts provided a chance to spend the winter together with him in Leicestershire. By Christmas nine of them – William, Mary, Dorothy, Johnny, Dora and Thomas Wordsworth, Coleridge and his elder son Hartley, and Sara Hutchinson – were all duly ensconced in a farmhouse near Coleorton Hall, the Beaumonts' stately home.

'*Peele Castle in a Storm*': Sir George Beaumont (Sir Francis Beaumont).

William Wordsworth: Henry Edridge, 1806
(Wordsworth Museum).

Thomas De Quincey: Sir John Watson Gordon
1788–1864 (Wordsworth Museum).

*Silhouette of Dorothy Wordsworth as a young
woman* (Wordsworth Museum).

1807

It was not until July that the family returned to Dove Cottage. The year had begun with William designing a 'Winter Garden' for Sir George in the daytime, and reading Coleridge *The Prelude* in the evening. He was delighted to be taken seriously as a gardener, and must also have been pleased by the response to the poem. Coleridge, in lines written (or begun) the night that the reading ceased, hailed *The Prelude* as 'A tale divine of high and passionate thoughts', and the poet himself as among 'the choir / Of ever enduring men . . . the truly great'.

Neither landscape-gardening, though, nor the acceptance of his poem, could make up for the loss of companionship. Since his return from Malta, Coleridge had withdrawn into himself. The sense of exclusion that everyone felt is recorded with a pained straightforwardness in Wordsworth's *Complaint*:

> There is a change, and I am poor:
> Your love hath been, nor long ago,
> A fountain at my fond heart's door . . .
> Now, for this consecrated fount
> Of murmuring, sparkling, living love,
> What have I? (Shall I dare to tell?)
> A comfortless, and hidden well.

A Complaint was published almost at once, among the *Poems in Two Volumes*, which appeared in April. To Lady Beaumont William claimed to have no care for his poems' immediate reception. 'Of what moment is that', he wrote, with a confidence worthy of Milton,

compared with what I trust is their destiny – to console the afflicted, to add sunshine to daylight by making the happy happier; to teach the young and the gracious of every age to see, to think, and feel . . .

The return to Grasmere was a sad one. Dorothy's first letter reads like a lament : 'On our arrival here our spirits sank, and our first walk in the evening was very melancholy. Many persons are dead. . . . All the trees in Bainriggs are cut down . . .' The children, though, were happy to be back in their old haunts – Dora (aged nearly three), who was 'of the dancing brood, and given to ecstasy' ; John (aged four), 'of a more sober and thoughtful nature, though very joyful' ; little Thomas (13 months), a 'stout healthy-faced child', almost able to walk. Dove Cottage was now decidedly too small. Arrangements had been made for the move to Allan Bank, on the other side of the vale, that would take place the following May. Meanwhile, Dove Cottage was to have one of its most important visitors.

Thomas De Quincey, famous later for his *Confessions of an English Opium-Eater*, finally arrived on 4 November. He had written to Wordsworth as early as May 1803 in terms of extravagant praise : the poet's genius, he said, was transcendent, wild, magnificent. Since then he had twice set out for Grasmere, but turned back because his courage failed him. Now, after four long years, he had come. Looking back, De Quincey, who was to be tenant of Dove Cottage in succession to the Wordsworths, gives us a marvellous picture of what it was like to cross the threshold that day in 1807.

First he sees Mary, but immediately behind is Dorothy – 'shorter, slighter . . . as different from her in personal characteristics as could have been wished for the most effective contrast. "Her face was of Egyptian brown". . . . Her eyes were not soft, as Mrs. Wordsworth's, nor were they fierce and bold, but they were wild and startling, and hurried in their motion.'

1808

The last six months at Dove Cottage were busy ones. Nobody wanted to move. In January, Dorothy tells Lady Beaumont, 'we are so glad that we are not in the *new* house that we are disposed to make the best of every thing and to fancy ourselves very comfortable'. Then she adds the detail that shows how much her life, and William's, has changed since the early days in the cottage before the poet's marriage:

Though I must confess we are never thoroughly so till after seven o'clock in the evening, when the children are put to bed, and the business of the house is over . . .

In February Wordsworth went down to London, where Coleridge believed himself to be dying, and was certainly taking too much opium. Once more the city in its early-morning peacefulness caught his imagination, as it had on Westminster Bridge in 1802:

I left Coleridge at 7 o'clock on Sunday morning, and walked towards the City . . . looking up, I saw before me the avenue of Fleet Street, silent, empty, and pure white, with a sprinkling of new-fallen snow, not a cart or carriage to obstruct the view, no noise, only a few soundless and dusky foot-passengers, here and there . . . you remember the elegant curve of Ludgate Hill . . . beyond and towering above it was the huge and majestic form of St Pauls, solemnised by a thin veil of falling snow.

Grasmere, meanwhile, was full of activity and anxiety. George Green and his wife Sarah had gone to a sale in Langdale, taken a short cut back over the fells, got lost in the snow, and fallen to their deaths. Their two eldest daughters were already in service – one at Dove Cottage – but the six youngest children, aged from eleven downwards, had waited two days in their tiny house in Easedale before going to look for help. Dorothy gives a vivid account before the bodies have even been found. Fifty to sixty men are out searching in heavy snow, while the women do their best to comfort the children – 'all wait with trembling and fear'.

The Greens were the poorest people in Grasmere; but, as 'statesmen', not labourers, they worked on their own land, and had that independence that Wordsworth above all valued. No one had known how poor they were. They had had to sell their horse; their cow was old; their land (like Michael's in the poem) was heavily mortgaged. The Parish voted two shillings a week maintenance for the younger children, but the Wordsworths soon found themselves campaigning to pay for their education.

Using what he terms 'a multiplying-writer', William sent out letters to his wealthier friends. He also wrote, to be used in the Appeal, his last Dove Cottage poem:

> Now do those sternly-featured hills
> Look gently on this grave,
> And quiet now is the depth of air
> As the sea without a wave.
>
> But deeper lies the heart of peace,
> In shelter more profound;
> The heart of quietness is here
> Within this churchyard-ground.

Those 'sternly-featured hills' of Grasmere had taken the lives of the Greens, just as the sea and its waves had taken that of John in 1805. The Dove Cottage years, 1799–1808, had been happy, creative, in many ways fulfilled, but Wordsworth's eye now was truly one that had 'kept watch o'er man's mortality'.

Watercolour by Joseph Farington, clearly showing Allan Bank high on the ridge to the right of the church, c. 1815 (Jonathan Wordsworth).

Mary Wordsworth, a photograph believed to date from the 1830s.

The happiness of the Dove Cottage years was never to be recaptured. William became a national figure, acknowledged by many as the greatest poet of his age. Distinguished visitors sought him out in his new, much larger home at Rydal Mount; the universities of Durham and Oxford granted him honorary degrees; in 1843 he became Poet Laureate. When he died, in 1850, the influence of his poetry was felt throughout the English-speaking world.

The later years, though, were darkened by many sadnesses. At Allan Bank, in 1810, came the bitter and unnecessary quarrel with Coleridge, which was patched up, but left everyone the poorer. At the Rectory, in 1812, two of the five children – Catharine and Thomas – died within six months of each other. In 1828 Dorothy became seriously ill. From 1835 she suffered from arterio-sclerosis, losing her memory, and crouching fretfully summer and winter over the fire, save when William pushed her in a wheel-chair round the garden. She did not die till 1855.

Like Margaret in *The Ruined Cottage*, William 'went struggling on through those calamitous years / With cheerful hope'. The move to Rydal in 1813 was followed by publication of *The Excursion*. Grieving over Catharine, he produced the touching sonnet, *Surprised by Joy*. As late as 1835 he could write the beautiful *Airey-Force Valley*. It is in the last of the *Duddon Sonnets* (1820), however, that we hear the voice of his resolve:

> We men, who in our morn of youth defied
> The elements, must vanish – be it so;
> Enough, if something from our hands have power
> To live, and act, and serve the future hour;
> And if, as toward the silent tomb we go,
> Through love, through hope, and faith's transcendent dower,
> We feel that we are greater than we know.